QUANTUM ENTANGLEMENT

QUANTUM ENTANGLEMENT

GARY REDDIN

Mouthfeel Press is an indie press publishing works in English and
Spanish by new and established writers. We publish poetry, fiction, and
non-fiction.

Cover Design: Enzo Rodríquez Suárez
Interior Design: Kimberly James

Contact Information:
Mouthfeelbooks.com
Info.mouthfeelbooks@gmail.com

Print ISBN: 978-1-957840-40-6

Published in the United States, 2025

$18

Acknowledgments

I have a confession. I never wanted to be a poet. Not in the traditional sense, I suppose. I wanted to be a writer, and poets were – for a long time – not on my radar as writers. And then I met Dr. John Graves Morris, Cameron University's pre-eminent poet. A man that I'm certain I drove a bit insane with my insistence for shirking any semblance of form and writing poetry with the ferocity of a racoon scrambling through the trash bins. But despite my distaste for pentameter or frankly the basic rules of grammar, he saw something in me. It's thanks to John that I fell in love with poetry and, were this book not dedicated to my wife, it would be dedicated to him. Along with several of my other professors including Dr. Bayard Godsave, who I wrote my first real poem under, Jenny Yang Cropp, who's beautiful collection "String Theory" partially inspired this collection, and George McCormick, who is probably disappointed that my first book isn't a novel, but, I hope, nonetheless proud. I also need to thank the team at Mouthfeel Press, for taking a chance on this strange amalgamation of science, poetry, and prose. And finally, to Danielle, who hates public displays of affection, I dedicate this book.

Contents

For Danielle

Uncertainty Principle

there are features of this universe
that cannot be known
with complete precision
positions and velocities
between two constants
an unpredictability of motion
as distance scales them
immeasurably closer
their particles dance
between every possibility

in a frenzied state
of uncertainty

Jellyfish

it is okay to feel lost
not like a broken compass
but like a jellyfish
soft and directionless
because
to be a jellyfish
is a miracle
the ocean
will drown the roots
that reach for you
and when you're ready
you can always find a way home
and even if you can't
you'll still be soft and brave
so stay lost
little jellyfish

Subatomic

on this level we can be anything

       our bones made of sweet sugarcane

the tendons that hold our structures together

       delicate feathers collected from a long walk

these muscles aching to hold our hearts in place

       nothing but honeysuckle, lavender, and oleander

we are amalgamations on the subatomic

       the button you lost from your sweater

a liter of light from the winter sun

       and the dust of every room we will ever lie in

          together

String Theory

I wonder if maybe
we have infinite selves
scattered across a million timelines
your hands softly kneading dough
so distracted in your reverie
that you forget to add the salt
it's okay I tell you
because somewhere out there
you remembered

One Life Pulled from the Infinite

I know nothing of summer
but imagine it like this
I sneak out the side door
my father's keys in hand
trying not to wake the neighbors
as I roar out of the driveway
Vandals screaming from the stereo
singing along off-key
and drive three towns over
not for drugs, or sex, or even rock and roll
but to escape the light pollution
so I can lie out on the hood
ignoring the pressure in the July air
and the wounds of the world
which seem like nothing at all

The Theory of Relativity

if you've ever wondered
about relativity
how time can move
in waves for some
and pulses for others
have an hour-long conversation
with someone you love
then sit through thirty minutes
of a speech
about the state of commerce
or ten minutes
of freeform jazz
and tell me then
that time
doesn't match the rhythm
of our patience

Don't Bury Me in Oklahoma

don't lay me down
under tornado green skies
but let me dust gentle
against oceans I've never seen

break my bones into fragments
and mosaic them into mountains
of granite and coal to build
into steel for cities

make me into marble floors
of foreign manors
or broken windows in abandoned
factories no longer turning
muscle and sinew into machine

scatter my teeth like birdseed
let me feed the robins
and the crows alike

give my cells to sing light
into the lines of new hands
trace the eyes of fresh faces
and save my heart only
for the red earth
and the wild winds

Biology

twitch
in the chest

fire
in the cheeks

Solnit called it blue
the endless distance
between two points

the ocean
a linen sky

call it poetry
but never write such a thing

oh cliché, cliché, cliché

but what's a cliché
if not the simplest
truth

Mercy from Ghosts

nostalgia
is a spectrum
that shades our memories
in colors softer
than they deserve
rounds out the hard edges
of our histories
and keeps us longing
for hues
of soft blue
and sunset pink
crossing our hearts
and asking
mercy from ghosts

The Art of Treason

For Anthony Bourdain

Tony said
to write is a treason
so I understand why
it's impossible
to create poetry

something will always be lost
in the translation
but still we write
because our treasonous hearts
have no other recourse

Phantom Limbs

I have never felt a phantom limb
never known the way
a hand removed of self
can still reach to grasp
the handle of a pistol
but I've felt a phantom muscle
a ghost eye in my head
just below the surface
in search of a new vision

Quantum Entanglement

when two particles
form a relationship
within the infinite
they become entwined
in such a way
that their quantum selves
cannot exist independently
of one another
this state is constant
across vast distances
of space and time

Environmental Science

it hasn't rained in a year
I've heard it said that this
is the driest it has ever been
but it is a desert
and if the sky
will not drown us here
then we can keep our heads
above water
forever

String Theory II

I am thinking about the tear in my jacket
how a needle could thread the seam
and pull the disparate pieces together
I wonder if it is the same for time
if we tear it open
looking for our infinite selves
could we sew it shut again
or should we enjoy the fraying edges
our fingers on the loose strings

how easily

          they

               could

                         unravel

Liminal Space

I don't know much
about liminal spaces
about words left unsaid
or reading between lines
but I know that time is relative
and between a question

and an answer
there lives a thousand lives

Apocrypha

I'm not keeping
any of these words
even though I know
that they'll linger
in the white space
just out of view
Julien lies and tells me
there is no glory in it
I know, I know
that's why I'm cutting them
and leaving only the gore

The National Geographic Article Claims that Spiders Have Dreams

if I could, I would tell the spiders that we dream too
that these gods of flesh, bone, and electricity
sleep

can you imagine what it's like
to spider dream
sitting on a gossamer throne and
plucking the threads of reality
and watching the stars fall

ash, ash, all of it ash
not stars at all but ash

and they see how we
gods of bone
can also bleed

and now, and now, and now
and now National Geographic tells me that scientists
have reanimated a spider's corpse
they call it necrobiotics
and I wonder, if the spiders dream
or wrack themselves with nightmares

Irregular Orbits

arrhythmic binary stars
caught in decaying orbit
their light will be scattered
into fractals too complex
for our distant geometry
so why are we afraid
of artificial satellites

A Song in The Dark of the Newborn Universe

light strummed a chord
across the strings of reality
and listened to echoes
keeping time in the dark
heard the drums
of creation
beat the newborn universe
to dust
if we can find harmony
in the dissonance
maybe there will be a song
somewhere in the vibration
of our molecules

Background Radiation

I think if it were possible
to get drunk on static
I would binge the noise
at the end of every record
the needle skipping softly
across the black vinyl
drink the cicada songs
from the summer night
take shots from the whispers
until my vision blurred
even if they ruined my liver
I'd drink until I blacked out

(No) Mercy from Ghosts

I've heard it said that hauntings
might just be the echoes
of other realities
so of course I worry
about the ghosts
of our infinite selves
when their echoes return
will they break my bones
and turn them into chains
rattling against the drywall
draped in the thin veil
we pulled over ourselves
to hide from the world
moving our chairs
throwing open our doors
showing our soft underbellies
to a bloodthirsty audience
ready to gut us
but will it even hurt
when they slip the knife
gently between my ribs
a delicate turn to nick the vein
that any ghost could be
so merciless

I Do Not Care About the State of Schrodinger's Cat

I've heard the theory about the cat
the one that is alive and dead
but I do not find it compelling
because this is the state of all things
we are stardust haunted by electricity
amalgamations of the dead
reconstituted and asked to care
about our new bodies
the way they move
in unfamiliar patterns
we are always coming back together
in this way
again and again
our cells are pulled
from the infinite

Gravitational Constants and an Inconsistency of Logic

the benefit of Newton's law
is that it allows us
to calculate
and more importantly
understand
the gravitational pull
between two constants
we use the language of math
to write a holy book
infallible
but what this religion of equations
does not account for
are the truths we find
in each other
the small moments of clarity
that exist in a shared cup of tea
or in knowing that
I do not think I believe
in an afterlife
but that I once lived
in a haunted house

Palmistry

you measure this ache
in the lines of your palms
the love and the life
you trace them
from hand to hand
across the skin
looking always
for where the horizons cross
into your other tomorrows

East Hope Road, Oklahoma

you drove east on a road called hope
knowing it would take you
to the anywhere of the in-between
you'd find a field and slip under the barbed wire
look for coyote tracks
wonder about alternate realities
decide that none of it really matters
because Emily told you once
that hope is the thing with feathers
and you can hear it singing its wordless song
a sparrow in some lonely willow
asking nothing of you

A Quiet Reclamation of Lost Things
For Faye

In a bath of quivering cricket song
I listen to the Ozark Elegy, a static
whisper at the edge of wild grief.

As the preacher starts in on hell
I am eaten by rage, and the hard
wooden hope of the pew.
Your name passes through
his swollen lips just once
before the brimstone.

I worry about the humidity
in this backwoods cemetery.
As the swell of wet earth under my feet
threatens to bring my ancestors
back as calcium flowers.

Meanwhile, men cut soft into the earth
to make you a final bed of mealworms and granite.
All in the shadows of these hills.
Their hands have forgotten
more work than mine
will ever know.
But in their mourning song,
I find a prayer.

A quiet reclamation of lost things.

Oklahoma State

State: "a complete description of the observable characteristics of a physical system"

I want to feel the deep red earth
guide our hands into this clay soil
that still echoes with tribal drums
find a twisted willow slowly dying
its guts spun 'round by a forgotten tornado
and climb its firm limbs
offer all these dying towns
one last kiss before their roots
pull themselves apart and turn to ghosts
run wild through the wheat fields
sending all the grasshoppers alight
to fill this starless sky
sit quiet on the shore of Eufaula
under a brass sun
taste fresh blackberries
keep calm as the wall clouds roll in
watch the sky bruise under a summer storm
feel the thunder in our ribcages
and remain in this state
forever

Chaos Theory

to pin a moth to a board
is a cruel exercise in causality
nothing like the metaphor
of a butterfly's wings
and a distant typhoon
the pinned moth cannot
affect the weather
across the ocean
its uneasy heart
pierced so thoughtlessly
its wings
shedding the dust
of our language
so much excess weight
what words we lose
once they've grown
still

Untethered

we are electrical impulses
trapped by flesh

I am not made
of singing electrons

but skin and bone and muscle

unconcerned
with gravity
untethered
from the earth

which is to say
weightless

Oklahoma Coast

you came to a field tricking reality
into believing there was an ocean among the red earth
and walked out into the water
the salt drying your skin like venison
wading until the coast disappeared drifting
into the waves of wheatgrass and stalking coyotes
adrift somewhere between the blue of the sea
and the sky until the prairie came roaring back
screaming like an angry thrashing child god
all wind and hail and drowning rains

To Prove a Miracle Empirically

we inspect it for bias
send our research for peer review
calculate probabilities
analyze their outcomes
the poets call us blind
to not recognize this truth
but poets do not require
physical evidence
to prove that love is a miracle
or sweat and lust
poets do not need to show
how grief and envy
can be the same emotion
or that longing
is no different
than the deep blue
of the middle distance

Light-Soaked Verse

spring
with all its needless empty gesture
opens its mouth
to sing and I remember
how the only songs I ever understood
were the ones about loss

fill my head with light-soaked verse
let me empty my tongue
of heathen curses
and praise this unending
restless season

I can be a pagan if you need
just promise me a new
pantheon when the sun
finally yawns out its ghosts
to haunt our hallowed veins
thirsty for a new god

Grief is a Yellow Thing

43

fuck the poem
that compares it
to a rose
the way they
both draw blood
what a desperate metaphor
grief is a yellow thing
stubborn and small
that can grow
from the hardest earth
the smallest crack
where the wind
scatters its seeds
so it finds purchase
in new ground
and grows again

A Breakfast of Ghosts

44

I will crack these rooms open like eggs
empty the yolk of ghosts into a bowl
why shouldn't I let this flesh go
you know I will say it's poetry
this frenzy of light
that leaks from carved distance
but don't pity the moth
that calls it a home
the truth is so simple
despite these soft fractals
these ghosts are a haunting

I've chosen to eat

Pythagoras at the Edge of the Universe
For Brandon

we speak in different tongues

yours a language
of numbers and lines
dividing out
the zeroes
into ones
this infallible
syntax

mine a staccato
of metaphor and verse
that pulls at disparate
strings of codes
to write
of religions
that do not
exist

yet yours
are the words
I would carve
in the flesh
of the infinite
to sing
at the edges

a hymn
in fractions

a sum greater
than the parts

Thermodynamics of the Summer Rebellions

they don't speak about burning
because they've never been on fire
but I have burned and charred
and my skin has ashed in the flame
of this thing
a time or two before

here I thought I was still burning

but they've shown me
that I am a pile of brush
stacked thick with dead wood

they don't speak about burning
because we are a match
they are the tinder
and god forgive us
the wildfire we'd spark
if they did

Synapses

I know that poetry
takes memory
turns it to epitaph
that words are not
chemistry
not subtle vibration
of atom
not electric signal
through wet flesh
bird on a live wire
hand touching warm stone
little pulses of light
what will remain of them
when they arrive

A Body at Rest

even the infinite self
needs rest
an echo to lay its head
down
and call it a
favor
a pause for reflection
when every moment
can feel like too much
and never enough
take me
my friend
for whatever you need
to keep yourself
from drowning
in sleep
and the pain
of living

Middle Distance

You could walk out into this field
the razor grass alive
despite the January frost
and wait for the sky
to tear itself open
and drown you whole
but I would worry
about the razor grass
and the winter flowers
because I know this sorrow
of yours
is only loneliness
and loneliness is not worth
the loss of something so resilient

Cell Death

a heart slips open
life's blood
sifting through her
torn seams
a poor surgeon
a poet makes
because darling
look what you're losing

String Theory Variations
For Danielle

we speak so often
of these enigmas
the lives we wish
we could live

but consider this
a variation on a theme

I would love you
in this life
and each one
between

Deep Field

points of light
like flowers
blooming
in cosmic comedy
as if to say
they do not care
about us
or the polished mirrors
we use to bend
wavelengths
long enough
to capture
in stillness
this image of
our distant past
an echo
a laugh

See Footnotes

For John Graves Morris

I'll never understand
why we edit poetry[1]
how writers can
clip the wings
and hide the fangs
of these wild,
wanting creatures
yearning to devour
their readers
and not let them
live as they were born

ravenous

---

1. This poem has been edited for clarity and length.

Object Permanence

54

when we were younger
we worried that the faces
of our parents would
abandon us
hidden behind hands
now wrinkled
and bruised
from IV needles
now we hope
that they do not fear
the same

Artificial Intelligence

So come then
cut down this heart noose
and drop our madness
to your floor
then tell me what dirt
a machine poet
can clean
from our filthy language

what does your artifice know
of heavy things
it could not hold
the weight
of this
wounded animal
or find its breath

in the white space

Superposition

we give names to storms
for the same reason we split the atom
to call out to the void
I am here
see me
but I am done naming storms
I will let the knife slide through the atom
unobserved
we can live out our lives
in superposition
settle our bones
into the spaces between
the known

comfortable in our quantum state

together among the infinite

Previously Published

Many of these poems found homes outside of this collection and I must thank the literary magazines, journals, and websites that provided them shelter.

"Jellyfish" originally appeared in *The Dillydoun Review.*

"String Theory I" and "One Life Pulled" from the Infinite originally appeared in *Cathexis Northwest Press.*

"Don't Bury Me in Oklahoma" originally appeared in *Drunk Monkeys.*

"Apocrypha" originally appeared in *The Oklahoma Review.*

"Uncertainty Principle," "Biology," and "The Art of Treason," appeared originally in *Black Stone/White Stone Review.*

About the Author

Gary Reddin grew up in Southwest Oklahoma, where he mythologized Springsteen lyrics as gospel truth. After nearly a decade in journalism, an MFA in writing, and a short, ill-advised journey into academia, he left one desert for another, following the love of his life to Southern California. These days he works as a writer and script editor for Complexly. His work has appeared in many places online and off – mostly off. He is also the author of *An Abridged History of American Violence*. He can be found everywhere online as @reddinwrites, though it's mostly pictures of his dog.